Serena Williams

A Little Golden Book® Biography

By Bria Alston

Illustrated by Anthony Ketuojor Ikediuba

g A GOLDEN BOOK • NEW YORK

Golden Books
An imprint of Random House Children's Books • A division of Penguin Random House LLC
1745 Broadway, New York, NY 10019 • penguinrandomhouse.com • rhcbooks.com
Text copyright © 2025 by Bria Alston
Cover art and interior illustrations copyright © 2025 by Anthony Ketuojor Ikediuba
Golden Books, A Golden Book, A Little Golden Book, the G colophon, and the distinctive gold
spine are registered trademarks of Penguin Random House LLC.
Library of Congress Control Number: 2024950006
ISBN 978-0-593-90446-6 (trade) — ISBN 978-0-593-90447-3 (ebook)
Manufactured in the United States of America
10 9 8 7 6 5 4 3 2 1
EU Contact: Penguin Random House Ireland, 32 Nassau Street, Dublin D02 YH68.
https://eu-contact.penguin.ie

Serena Jameka Williams was born September 26, 1981, in Saginaw, Michigan. A few years later, her father, Richard, and mother, Oracene, moved the family to Compton, California. Serena shared a bedroom with her four older sisters.

Compton was a dangerous neighborhood. Serena's dad was always looking for a way to give his family a better life.

Richard decided that his two youngest girls—Venus and Serena—would one day be tennis champions. First, he taught himself how to play tennis by watching videos and reading books. Then, when Serena was just three years old and Venus was four, he started teaching them.

Even as a little girl, Serena wanted to be the best at whatever she did. Her big sisters let her win at card games and family talent shows because she didn't like to lose.

Serena had that same desire to win every time she stepped onto a tennis court.

She and Venus worked hard, playing on the neighborhood courts with their father six days a week. They came with a shopping cart full of tennis balls. Their older sisters would gather the balls so Serena and Venus could keep practicing.

Serena competed in her first junior tournament when she was nine years old. She made it to the final round—and so did Venus! Her big sister won that match.

Soon, people everywhere were talking about the talented young Black girls from Compton. They were interviewed on TV and featured in newspaper and magazine articles.

Tennis was a big part of Serena's life, but her parents made sure that she had time to be a regular kid. And she and Venus weren't allowed to play tennis if they didn't finish their schoolwork.

In 1991, the whole family moved to Florida so Serena and Venus could train at Rick Macci's Tennis Academy. Coach Macci was impressed by the girls' powerful serves and their speed.

But their training involved more than just hitting balls on the tennis court. They also did ballet, gymnastics, and boxing.

In 1995, at the age of fourteen, Serena became a professional tennis player. Her first pro match was at the Bell Challenge in Quebec, Canada. She lost in the first round.

She kept training hard and improving her game. In 1998, Serena played in the Australian Open. It was her first major tournament, also called a Grand Slam. She made it to the second round but ended up losing that match to her sister.

Serena won the US Open in 1999, when she was seventeen years old. She was the first Black woman to win since Althea Gibson in 1958. This was Serena's first Grand Slam championship. It would not be her last!

From 2002 to 2003, she won all four Grand Slam titles—the French Open, Wimbledon, the US Open, and the Australian Open. People called it the Serena Slam.

In September 2003, Serena's oldest sister, Yetunde Price, was a victim of gun violence. It was hard to play tennis while feeling so sad. She began losing matches. She went from being the number one player in the world to number 140—but she didn't give up. Serena won the Australian Open in 2007 and dedicated the win to Yetunde.

Serena has spoken out against guns and racism. And she has helped children around the world get a good education by building schools in Jamaica and Africa, and by paying for college scholarships in the United States.

Serena wasn't only a top singles tennis player—she and Venus teamed up to play doubles. Together, they won doubles titles in fourteen Grand Slam tournaments. They also won the gold medal at the Olympics in 2000, 2008, and 2012!

Serena's style helped set her apart from other tennis players. She has stepped onto the court wearing colorful catsuits, denim skirts, and even tutus!

Serena attended fashion school and created her own clothing line called S by Serena. She makes clothes that help people look and feel confident, no matter what size they are. She also designs jewelry.

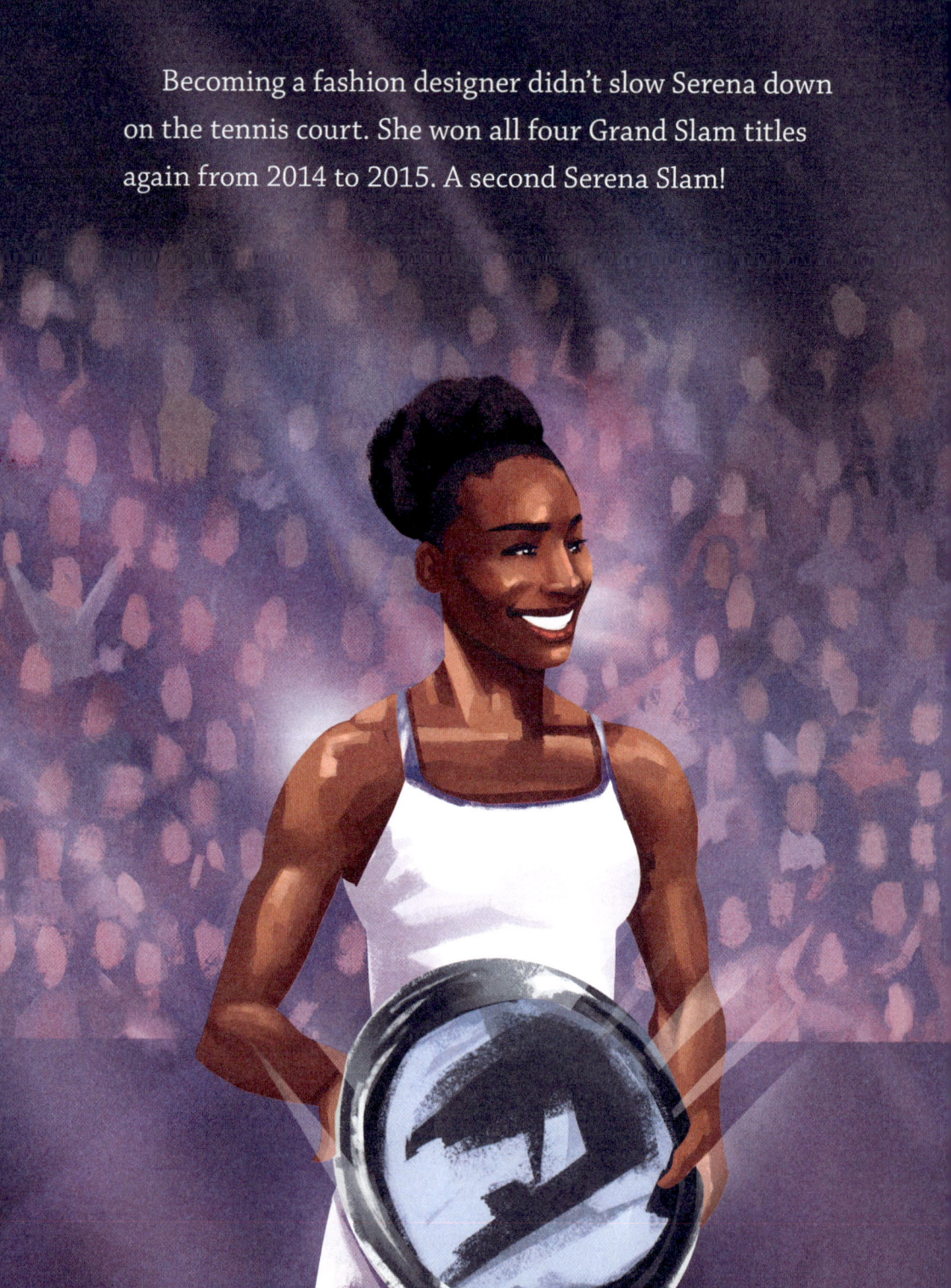

Becoming a fashion designer didn't slow Serena down on the tennis court. She won all four Grand Slam titles again from 2014 to 2015. A second Serena Slam!

Then, on January 28, 2017, Serena made history when she defeated Venus and won the Australian Open. It was Serena's 23rd Grand Slam title—a new record for the most Grand Slam singles titles won by any player! At thirty-five years old, Serena also became the oldest woman to win a Grand Slam.

Serena's family is the most important thing to her. She and her husband, Alexis Ohanian, have two daughters, Olympia and Adira.

Serena enjoys volunteering at their school and having princess dance parties with her girls.

In August of 2022, Serena announced that she would stop playing professional tennis after that year's US Open. More than 4.8 million viewers watched her final match against Ajla Tomljanović in the tournament's third round.

In an emotional speech afterward, she thanked her older sister for all her love and support. "I wouldn't be Serena if there wasn't Venus."

Serena Williams is considered one of the best tennis players of all time. She changed the sport with her power, strength, and style. Serena has inspired people around the world, especially Black girls, to follow their dreams and never give up.